Presented to

_____

_____

*On this*_____*day of*_____

*By*_____

_____

Published AD 2007 by:

P.O Box 5296
Chullora NSW 2190 AUSTRALIA
Tel (+61 2) 9742 5716; Fax (+61 2) 9742 5715
Website: www.amazinggrace.org.au
Email: info@amazinggrace.org.au

All Scripture quotations are from the Authorised King James Version.

All quotes with a page number only e.g. (P.?) are from the book "Out of the Depths –
An Autobiography of John Newton". Otherwise as noted.

ISBN 978-0-9803391-0-9

First Printing 10,000 - April 2007
Second Printing 10,000 - November 2007

Printed By Rainbow Printing Pty Ltd
Units 1&2/3 Muir Place. Wetherill Park, NSW 2164
Phone: 02 9725 2500
Fax: 02 9725 4936
sales@rainbowprinting.com.au
www.rainbowprinting.com.au

Cover design by Joe Attwater

'The Man & The Story Behind Amazing Grace' is also available as an abridged gospel
tract, in audio format, and as an A3 poster (see page 83 to order).

Amazing Grace

Amazing grace ! (how sweet the sound)
that saved a wretch like me !
I once was lost but now am found,
was blind but now I see ...

John Newton

Peter Rahme

Acknowledgements

I found the following references very helpful,
in particular Mr Turner's latest research:

Noel Davidson
How Sweet *the* Sound (Ambassador 1997)

N. K. Macintosh
The Reverend Richard Johnson (Pilgrim International Limited 1975)

Brian H.Edwards
Through Many Dangers-The story of John Newton
(Evangelical Press 1975)

Steve Turner
Amazing Grace -The Story of America's Most Beloved Song
(Harper Collins 2002)

The last two resources are absolute priceless treasures. As you will see,
I have relied heavily on and referred extensively to them:

Richard Cecil - edited and updated by Marylynn Rouse
The Life of John Newton - Authorised Biography (Christian Focus 2000)

John Newton
Out Of The Depths - An Autobiography (Kregel Publications 1990)

Also my sincere thanks to …

Michael Reed - Grave site photo
Roslyn & David Phillips - Other photos
Faith Rahme, Margaret Gorle, Merle Mitchell, Angela Chappell & Armen Gakavian
- proofreading

Dedicated to...

The Lord Jesus Christ
My gracious Saviour

John and **Sara**
My handsome Father and beautiful late Mother

Faith
My darling Wife

Todd and *Lissa*, **Melodie** and *Dave*, and **Amira-Faith**
My wonderful Children and *their lovely Spouses*

Georgia, Savannah, Jackson and **Xavier**
My *great* Grandchildren

Inner West Baptist Church
My first Church

I want the whole world to know how much I love you!!!

Endorsements & Support

"Peter Rahme, a precious brother in the Lord and a very dear friend, is multi-talented, enthusiastic and contagious in his faith and an effective communicator of the Gospel through his words and deeds. He has graphically shown in The Man and the Story Behind Amazing Grace, how God's Grace can transform a blaspheming slave trader into a monumental saint who influenced many lives and contributed to the abolition of slavery. The book is quite challenging and engaging, and I endorse and recommend that everyone should read it"

Daniel Scot - Ibrahim Ministries International

"Peter Rahme has a deep desire and yearning to share the facts, figures and details in an easily understood fashion, regarding his heartfelt beliefs and the foundations for his Christian beliefs. His latest publication "The Man & The Story Behind Amazing Grace" is no exception. We know the tune, the words and some are aware of the composer of "Amazing Grace", but Peter has introduced us to the family background, the steps leading to a changed life and the ways in which the Lord can guide and direct a life given over to Him. John Newton's background and experiences could equate with many reading these words. Thank you Peter for sharing with us something of your research and depth of knowledge regarding The Man and The Story Behind Amazing Grace."

Ramon A. Williams - Journalist and photographer
World Wide Photos, the Religious Media Agency

"2007 will be the bicentenary of two important events - the death of John Newton, and the abolition of the slave trade by the British parliament. Hopefully, this may prove enough incentive for people to want to know more about the converted slave trader, John Newton, and his experience of amazing grace. Peter Rahme wrote a most helpful booklet on Mr Eternity, and he has followed this up with an equally helpful work on John Newton. It is warmly commended to readers. "

Rev. Dr. Peter Barnes
Lecturer in Church History, Presbyterian Theological Centre

"Perhaps you have sung the song "Amazing Grace" many times but now you can read the inspiring story of the life changing encounter the writer had with Jesus Christ that inspired the much loved words of the song. This story of the life of John Newton will challenge you to consider your own walk with God and how you might avail yourself of His Amazing Grace."

Brian Pickering - National Coordinator, Australian Prayer Network

"Peter Rahme is a man and a steward of God, with talents and influence. May God bless this book for the benefit of many in the years to come"

Colman Chan. - CEO, Christian Life Mission
Publisher, Life Monthly

"Rahme's retelling of the life of John Newton and the writing of Amazing Grace is both poignant and captivating. Anyone who has ever sung the song will be touched by the pathos of Newton's story. Anyone who has experienced God's Amazing Grace will once again be led to remember his own journey from bondage to freedom. The story of Newton and the world's best-loved hymn is always worth retelling. Well Done!"

Pastor Phil Waters - Grace Baptist Church

"In both this book and the Gospel leaflet "The man and the story behind Amazing Grace", Peter Rahme shows God's rich love to John Newton in "saving a wretch like him". We all know we are just like John Newton in heart if not also in action. We have broken God's laws too! That is why the song "Amazing Grace" has touched and still touches so many lives. I highly endorse and recommend this book to you because in it, without much difficulty, you too will discover the "real" author of "Amazing Grace". (Our Amazing Saviour, the Lord Jesus Christ)."

Rev. David Knight -Teach and Tell Ministries

"Throughout the history of mankind grace has set free countless people so that their ultimate treasure in life would be the God of all grace. Peter shares his love for the transformational story surrounding the man who is known to have penned the beloved song, 'Amazing Grace'; but more than that he reveals his radical abandonment to the God from whom this grace so freely flows."

Pastor Kirby Lancaster - South Valley Baptist Church

"A gift most appreciated is a gift that meets the greatest need. Peter Rahme succinctly tells of John Newton's recognition of his greatest need and how he called upon Jesus Christ to meet that need. This is a timeless story, one that is always relevant. Thank you Peter Rahme for telling us about the "The Man and the Story Behind Amazing Grace".

Daniel Keegan - Director, Word of Life Australia

"An inspiring book on heroes of the faith, revealing God's graciousness. We need more books like this."

Graham McLennan – Chairman, National Alliance of Christian Leaders

'In this book Peter Rahme presents an engaging and readable account of the life and work of John Newton. From the words of the well-known hymn Amazing Grace, describing Newton's heart-felt emotions after his dramatic conversion, to the account of his life as a minister of religion and the battle to abolish slavery, the facts of the story are clearly laid out. The role of John Newton in sending Rev. Richard Johnson to Australia as chaplain on the First Fleet is also documented. The book is timely as we celebrate the 200th anniversary of the abolition of the slave trade by the British Empire during 2007. Well worth reading!"*

Peter & Jenny Stokes – Founders, Salt Shakers

"As an indigenous Australian discovering the wonderful grace of GOD through Christ my Saviour has been a life changing experience for me. We have always sung this hymn Amazing Grace at funerals without fully knowing the story behind both the hymn writer and the hymn. Thanks to Pastor Peter Rahme. I now fully appreciate the spiritual significance of the words in John Newton's life ... Now this hymn will always have a profound meaning when we consider the transformed life of the John Newton when he came to understand the mercy and grace of Almighty GOD."*

Harold Stewart - Principal Aboriginal Mental Health Consultant

"The lives of great Christian believers in past centuries have the potential for influencing and guiding and inspiring those of us who live in the early years of the Third Millennium AD. They can be a particular challenge to our youth. As with his book on Arthur Stace – "Mr Eternity" – Pastor Peter Rahme, employs inimitable enthusiasm, and passion, but with historical accuracy and spiritual discernment, to bring to us aspects of the life of a sea-farer and slave trader John Newton and the events which led to his conversion of Christianity and the writing of "Amazing Grace". It is a great read for you and every member of your family."*

Visiting Professor Leslie Kemeny - The Australian Foundation Member
Of the International Nuclear Energy Academy

"Reading Peter's new book reminds me, once again, not only of God's "Amazing Grace", but also the incredible potential there is for each one of us, who believe and obey, to make a significant impact on our own generation and in fact on generations to come ... My hope and prayer is that many will be encouraged through this publication, but most of all that many will take to heart Peter's concluding challenge and accept for themselves this "Amazing Grace", be converted to Christ and receive eternal life."*

Robin J Johnson - Senior Minister: Encounter Craigieburn AOG
Founder & President Joseph Publishing & Media Inc

"If there is a word that could describe Peter Rahme it is passion. He is passionate about his faith and making it known and this comes out in his latest book on the life of John Newton. True to form Peter is keen for his readers to realise the amazing story behind John Newton's most famous and enduring song Amazing Grace. As he states it has been sung and recorded by many but often without understanding the incredible story behind it. As you read this book you will be left in no doubt that we have a wonderful God who saves to the uttermost the most unlikely people, and that daily we experience God's amazing grace."

Carl Carmody - Publisher, Challenge Good News Paper

"Life touches Life; and Peter Rahme's life in Christ, has touched my life with his ministry and song, and it gives me great pleasure to commend and support Peter's writings on the life of John Newton, in whom the Lord God, glorifies Jesus Christ, within John Newton's personal life and song, Amazing Grace, through which the Gospel of God's Grace is made known through out the all ages."

Pastor Ossie Cruse MBE AM - Aboriginal Evangelical Church Eden

"What an amazing man to write about! What a wonderful subject to touch with a mortal pen! Thank you Peter for deciding to bring more light of this fascinating story. Amazing grace and John Newton are an inseparable duet, making music in the chorus of God's eternal choir."

Rev. Steven Kasambalis - Mt Waverley Community Church of the Nazarene

"On this historical anniversary of the abolition of slavery, Peter Rahme has provided an eloquent, concise insight into the life of a great man of God who was at the centre of it all. John Newton's life and legacy are a testimony to faith in action. Newton's revulsion over his life as a sinner, and his commitment to the saving grace of Jesus Christ, are a challenge to us in this cold, selfish age."

Dr Armen Gakavian - lecturer, Macquarie Christian Studies Institute

Contents

Foreword

By The Reverend Honourable Fred Nile MLC

I am honoured to write this Foreword for Pastor Peter Rahme's tribute to John Newton's amazing hymn – Amazing Grace.

Peter, through his own personal faith in Jesus Christ, has developed a unique ability to convey God's saving work of grace in people's lives.

Peter lifted up Jesus Christ as Saviour when he recorded God's gift of grace at work in Arthur Stace's life – known as "Mr Eternity" and as presented in the subsequent film. Peter now has achieved the same spiritual success with this new publication of the story of the world famous hymn Amazing Grace and its author John Newton.

The amazing message of Peter's book is the way Almighty God uses the lives of the disciples of Jesus Christ in ways past their own human understanding.

My own life, like that of Arthur Stace, was dramatically changed by the preaching of the evangelist John Ridley, in January 1955, but I had no idea where my decision to give my life completely to Christ as my Lord and Saviour would lead - my willingness to die for Christ!

Now by the grace of God I have been privileged, like William Wilberforce, to serve for 25 years as Christ's servant in the NSW Parliament.

John Newton also had a powerful influence on William Wilberforce and inspired his successful 20-year campaign, in the British House of Commons, to set the slaves free throughout the British Empire to stop slave trading.

William Wilberforce's example as a Christian Member of Parliament has been an inspiration and model for my own life. I still remember the strange event where two distinguished British Government delegates from London came to the NSW Parliament and asked to see me. They said we have come to meet you, "Australia's William Wilberforce", and presented me with his life story. They then left me for important British Commonwealth meetings.

John Newton's other amazing influence is his impact on Reverend Richard Johnson, with his visionary proposal that he be the Chaplain and missionary of the First Fleet to Australia, landing on 26th January 1788 and which we celebrate each year on Australia Day.

So we thank Almighty God for the life of John Newton and his inspiring hymn, which has become the world's most popular hymn, yet conveys such a simple message that touches the hearts of rich and poor, high and low – "Amazing Grace! – how sweet the sound, that saved a wretch like me. I once was lost but now am found, was blind but now I see".

May Peter's message help others to experience the saving Grace of our Lord Jesus Christ.

-Fred Nile

Preface

Grace! What an amazingly sweet and a wonderfully rich word that blesses the human vocabulary. Whilst its unsearchable riches makes it hard to define and harder to describe, its unconditional love makes it simple to believe and simpler to receive.

Grace! What a rich possession and a regal position, though it can never be bought from anyone with any amount of money, yet it can be sought from God by a simple faith.

Grace! This single and simple word woos its way and weaves its wonder into a myriad of scenarios. It is...

Seen printed on letterheads, work uniforms and tee shirts.

Spoken of as a period of time extended in the fine print on the final page of a contract.

It is also a...

Sign placed on street corners and shopping complexes and featured on front doors, window cells and rooftops of homes, churches and even family enterprises.

Sacrilege title exercised inappropriately by religious and civic leaders.

Grace! This unique and unusual expression of the soul wears many hats and warms meek hearts. It is...

Sought from God - the Sovereign, the Healer and the Infinite Creator, by men and women - the sinful, hopeless and finite creature.

Said as a prayer of thanksgiving expressed to God at mealtime in recognition for His presence and provision.

It is also a...

Sweet name given to girls at birth in anticipation of their beauty and behaviour.

Song - John Newton's personal testimony and passionate tribute to God's Amazing Grace.

This book is all about *that Amazing Song*.

I trust as you read this condensed but comprehensive historical account of the soul of John Newton and the story of his Amazing Grace, you will also realise that what John Newton experienced there and then can also be yours here and now.

For your convenience, I have included book and Scripture references.

**What Mr. Eternity was to Sydney,
Amazing Grace is to the world!**

This was the seed that God planted in the soil of my heart in 2002, following *The Life & Legacy Of Mr Eternity's* successful campaign, which, after more than 3 years of 'work and labour of love', brought forth the fruit of *The Man & The Story Behind Amazing Grace*. Enjoy!

With the love of Christ
Peter Rahme
Sydney Australia

John Newton

AMAZING GRACE

"Amazing grace! (how sweet the sound)
that sav'd a wretch like me!
I once was lost but now am found,
was blind but now I see.
'T was grace that taught my heart to fear,
and grace my fears reliev'd;
How precious did that grace appear,
the hour I first believ'd!
The Lord has promis'd good to me,
His word my hope secures;
He will my shield and portion be,
as long as life endures.
Thru many dangers, toils, and snares,
I have already come;
'T is grace hath brought me safe thus far,
and grace will lead me home.
Yes, when this flesh and heart shall fail,
and mortal life shall cease;
I shall possess, within the vail,
a life of joy and peace.
The earth shall soon dissolve like snow,
the sun forbear to shine;
But God, who call'd me here below,
Will be forever mine."

John Newton

1. Magnificent Statistics

Amazing Grace has proven to be the most popular song of our time, from the church sphere to cyber space.

Its simple style is sought from varied sources; its sweet sound is found in a variety of situations:

> *From* the president's acceptance speech *to* the preacher's anointed sermon;
> *From* the simple harmonica in the rural outback *to* the stately harp in royal operas;
> *From* the first rejoicing moments of weddings *to* the final reflective minutes of funerals;
> *From* the moving stories on the small TV *to* the motion pictures on the big silver screen;
> *From* the tiny tune of a mobile phone *to* the powerful production of an Olympic ceremony;
> *From* the slide guitar of the American blues *to* the sustained notes of the Scottish bagpipes.

Amazing Grace is hummed and heard on every continent in this world!

It transcends race, religion and even record categories. It takes in its stride all nations, regardless of colour, creed or culture.

Whether presented in churches, performed in concerts or played in clubs, this song of songs touches the hearts of those who listen to its tune and learn its truth: this hymn of hymns transforms the souls of those who hear its message and heed its meaning.

Amazing Grace is high on the list of movie studios! The long index of films that have included its powerful presence is a testimony to its enduring power and remarkable popularity in the entertainment world.

Perhaps the most famous is *Brave Heart*, with its use of the bagpipes. Here is a brief list of other films, compiled by Steve Turner, that featured Amazing Grace:

Alice's Restaurant (1969)

Invasion of the Body Snatchers (1978)

Coal Miner's Daughter (1980)

Star Trek II (1982)

Silkwood (1983)

Dudes (1988)

The Handmaids Tale (1990)

Memphis Belle (1991)

Cry, The Beloved Country (1985)

Entertaining Angels (1996)

(Amazing Grace - Steve Turner P.227)

In addition, almost every funeral scene in movies has the accompanying background of the reassuring melody and comforting sound of Amazing Grace.

Amazing Grace is a hit on the music scene! Major artists, whether secular or spiritual, on stage or in the studio, have at some time referred to, rehearsed or recorded Amazing Grace as a solo project or with a strong choir - with over 2,000 different releases currently available.

Here is a list of some of the artists who recorded Amazing Grace:

Boys ll Men, Dave Matthews Band, Whitney Houston, Jerry Garcia & David Grisman, Tori Amos, Faith Evans, Twila Paris, Krystal, Glen Campbell, LeAnn Rimes, Janis Joplin, Shirley Caesar, Stevie Ray Vaughn, Paul Simon, Elvis Presley, Randy Travis, Arlo Guthrie,

101 Strings Orchestra, Chet Atkins, Seven Nations, Phil Driscoll, The Von Trapp Children, Victor Wooten, Jimmy Hendrix, Blind Boys of Alabama, Jordanaires, Meadowlark Lemon, Ani DiFranco, Royal Scots Dragoon Guards, Drop Kick Murphy, Aretha Franklin, Christy Lane, Conway Twitty, Andy Williams, Ladysmith Black Mambazo, Boots Randolph, Judy Collins, Mahalia Jackson, Batmobile, Vicky Philips, Blind Willie McTell, Sonny James, Lou Rawls, Pete Seeger, Esteban, Dropkick Murphys, Charlie Rich, Charlotte Church, Crazy Cat George, Johnny Cash, Original Drifters, Pat Boone, Mickey Gilley, Anne Murray, Joan Baez, Tommy Smith, Jim Nabors, Al Green, Shanon, Loretta Lynn, B.J. Thomas, Charlie Daniels Band, Ike & Tina Turner, Cherry Bomb Club, Pras -Ghetto ,Supastar Mantovani, Willie Nelson, Diana Ross, Patti Page, The Neville Brothers, Fats Domino, George Jones, Merle Haggard, Herbie Mann, Cincinnati Pops, Robert Shaw Festival Singers, George Gershwin, Elmer Bernstein, Voices of Watts, The Beat Daddys, Leadbelly, Andrew Lloyd Webber, The David Rose Orchestra, Lawrence Welk, K.C. & the Sunshine Band, Ray Stevens, The Weavers, The Lemonheads, Ray Price, Gatlin Brothers, Tsa'Ne Dose, Glenn Yarbrough, Scott Fitzgerald, Rod Stewart, Glenn Miller, Cecelia, Oak Ridge Boys...
(Source Unknown)

....

~ 23 ~

AMAZING GRACE

*"My mother, as I have heard from many,
was a pious, experienced Christian:
She was a Dissenter,
in communion with the late Dr. Jennings.*

*I was her only child; she was of a weak constitution,
and a retired temper (rather shy).*

*Almost her whole employment was the care of my education.
I have some faint remembrance of her care and instructions.
At no more than three years of age, she herself taught me English.*

*When I was four years old I could read with propriety
in any common book. She stored my memory,
which was then very retentive, with many valuable pieces,
chapters, and portions of Scripture, catechisms, hymns and poems.*

*My dear mother, besides the pains she took with me,
often commended me with many prayers and tears to God."*

John Newton

(P.21-22)

2. Mother and Son

Perhaps the saying 'Behind every great man there is a great woman' should be expanded to 'Behind every great man there are two great women: his mother and his wife.' This is certainly true in the case of John Newton.

The story of the man behind Amazing Grace begins with his mother, a woman of great faith.

Elizabeth Newton (nee Seatliffe) of Stepney was born in 1705 at Chatham, England.

At the tender young age of nineteen, she married Captain John Newton on September 24, 1724, at the St. Mary-le-bow Church.

The following year, when Elizabeth was twenty, baby Johnny was born on July 24, 1725 in Wapping. (Captain James Cook came to Wapping in 1764 to do his apprenticeship with a local shipowner).

On March 30, 1727, Elizabeth Newton became a member of a small independent chapel, a nonconformist congregation in Old Gravel Lane, Wapping New Stairs.

Her pastor, Dr. David Jennings (1691-1762), an able communicator, was a close friend of Isaac Watts (the well known hymn writer); Samuel Brewer (who helped establish Newton in the Christian faith after his conversion); and Phillip Dodridge (who won William Wilberforce to Christ).

This young mum raised little junior pretty much on her own. Her husband, a commander in the Mediterranean trade, was away at sea most of the time. Her parenting approach was simple and straight forward:
> She trusted God and prayed for her boy fervently;
> She took her son to church regularly;
> She taught him to read and write early.

In 1732, at the age of twenty-seven, and just thirteen days before John's seventh birthday, his devout mother and dedicated mentor died of tuberculosis, in the home of George and Elizabeth Catlett (their daughter Mary–Polly later became John's wife), Chatham, Kent.

Her absence left a big void in the boy's young heart in that he no longer had access to her good instructions, and he lived from then on without her godly influence.

The following year his father remarried. His new wife, Thomasina, a daughter of a substantial grazier from Aveley, bore him two sons, William and Henry, and a daughter Thomasina. The step mother had no interest in spiritual things. John wrote:

> *"...(she) lived many years, without the least thought of religion, never going so much as to a place of worship, except for the birth of a child."* (John Newton by Richard Cecil P.316)

The distant heart behind the different hands sent the young boy away to a boarding school in Stratford, Essex, for two years until the young lad eventually left there in his tenth year.

When Johnny was only eleven, his sailor father took him on his maiden sea voyage. Expected to follow in his dad's footsteps, he made several more trips over the next seven years. In regard to his distant father, John wrote:

> *"A man of remarkable good sense, and great knowledge of the world, he took great care of my morals. But he could not supply my mother's part. Having been educated in Spain, he always observed an air of distance and severity in his carriage (manner), which overawed and discouraged my spirit. I was always in fear before him, and therefore he had the less influence."* (P.23)

....

Train up a child in the way he should go:

and when he is old,

he will not depart from it.

Proverbs 22:6

(One of Elizabeth Newton's favourite proverbs)

AMAZING GRACE

"….I had not the least fear of God before my eyes,
nor the least sensibility of conscience.
I was possessed of so strong a spirit of delusion that I believed my own
lie and firmly persuaded that after death I should cease to be"

…I was exceedingly vile indeed…
I not only sinned with a high hand,
but made it my study to tempt and seduce others upon every occasion…

…my life, when awake,
was a course of most horrid impiety and profaneness.
I know not that I have ever since met so daring a blasphemer.
Not content with common oaths and imprecations,
I daily invented new ones …"

John Newton

(P.43; 46-47; 65)

3. Man of the Sea

In 1744, the French fleet was hovering at England's coast and war was imminent. John, a confused adolescent, was lost, lonely and on the loose. Due to his 'thoughtless conduct' the young seaman was press-ganged, on board HMS 'Harwich', at the Nore, a man-of-war.

The weight of navy life was too heavy for this frustrated teenager to carry. Unable to hold up under the strain of its rigid discipline and unwilling to handle the stresses of its daily routine, he eventually deserted ship.

He was soon found, sent back, stripped and severely flogged. Filled with bitter rage and full of black despair, the defiant sailor, now a demoted midshipman, was desperate to leave the navy altogether. His desire was for a less restricting way of life and more rewarding work and labour.

To his surprise and absolute delight, after weeks of solitary confinement, he was discharged unexpectedly from the British Royal Navy and dispatched onto a slave trading ship at the island of Madeira. John wrote:

> "...Upon inquiring, I was informed, that two men, from a Guinea ship, which lay near us, had entered on board the Harwich, and that the commodore, Sir George Pocock, had ordered the captain to send two others in their room. My heart instantly burned like fire. I begged the boat might be detained a few minutes: I ran to the lieutenant, and entreated him to intercede with the captain that I might be dismissed. Though I had been formally upon ill terms with these officers, and had disobliged them all in their turns, yet they had pitied my case, and were ready to serve me now. The Captain, who, when we were at Plymouth, had refused to exchange me at the request of Admiral Medley, was now easily prevailed on. In little more than half an hour from my being asleep in bed, I saw myself discharged, and safe on board another ship." (P.44)

Having abandoned his mother's early religious instructions, and accepted the values of an aggressive atheist, John accumulated the vocabulary of a blatant blasphemer. The angry young man, who neither feared God nor considered others, had degenerated into a vile and vulgar character with a mean and miserable lifestyle.

However, the sun was not to rise on his better days, as he had hoped, until the darkness of bitter nights had come to pass. After he had enjoyed six months of freedom on the open sea, the twenty-year-old was to endure one long year of captivity in West Africa.

This took place on Plantain Island, off the coast of Sierra Leone. There, his dream of work and wealth turned into a nightmare of sickness and starvation while he served a cold-hearted English master, and suffered at the cruel hands of his African mistress. He wrote,

> *"My new master... was much under the direction of a black woman, who lived with him as a wife. The woman, I know not for what reason, was strangely prejudiced against me from the first. What made it still worse for me was a severe illness which attacked me very soon, before I had opportunity to show what I could or would do in his service... I had sometimes not a little difficulty to procure a draught of cold water when burning with a fever. My bed was a mat spread upon a board or chest, and a log of wood was my pillow... My distress has been at times so great as to compel me to go by night and pull up roots in the plantation… These I have eaten raw upon the spot, for fear of discovery..."* (P.52-53)

'Destitute of food and clothing' and 'depressed to a degree beyond wretchedness', he wrote to his father seeking help and assistance. His father responded favourably and organised for a British merchant ship to bring his lost son home.

Meanwhile John's situation improved slightly as he 'obtained his master's consent to live with another trader on the island'.

Then in February 1747, in a remarkable sovereign set of events, the commander of 'the ship that had orders to bring him home' rescued Newton from the island, ending his fifteen months of unforgettable captivity.

....

THE MAN & THE STORY BEHIND
AMAZING GRACE

"March 21 is a day to be remembered by me.
I have never suffered it to pass wholly unnoticed since the year 1748.
On that day the Lord sent from on high
and delivered me out of deep waters.
I continued at the pump
from three in the morning till near noon,
and then I could no more.
I went and lay down upon my bed, uncertain,
and almost indifferent, whether I should rise again.
In an hour's time I was called.
Not being able to pump, I went to the helm,
and steered till midnight,
expecting a short interval for refreshment.
I had here leisure and opportunity to think
of my former religious professions,
the calls, warnings, and deliverances I had met with,
the licentious course of my life, particularly my unparalleled effrontery
in making the gospel the subject of ridicule.
I thought, allowing the Scripture premises, there never was,
nor could be, such a sinner as myself."

John Newton
(P.73)

4. Mercy in the Storm

At the age of twenty two, John, a wretched sinner, was converted from a daring blasphemer of God into a devout believer in Christ. He wrote:

> *"But let me not fail to praise that grace which could pardon, that blood which could expiate, such sins as mine. Yea, the Ethiopian may change his skin and the leopard his spots. I, who was the willing slave of every evil, possessed with a legion of unclean spirits, have been spared and saved, and changed, to stand as a monument of His almighty power for ever."* (P.47)

The three-fold lifeline God used to reach his dark heart and rescue his dear soul was:

The memory of his godly mother and her early input of Scripture;

The meaningful love for Mary Catlett, his sweetheart, whom he married two years later;

The messages of the Prodigal Son, Bishop Beveridge's sermons, and Stanhope's Thomas à Kempis' 'Of the Imitation of Christ'.

His 'great deliverance' took place one stormy night on March 21, 1748, whilst returning to England, on a cargo ship as a passenger, having being rescued from Africa.

He, the captain and a crew of ten were caught in a fierce storm which lasted on and off for eleven days.

The ship, carrying 'a great quantity of bees wax, wood' and 'live stock of pigs, sheep and poultry', was battered by monstrous winds and beaten by mountainous waves.

The tired sailors, like their torn sails, were helpless as they battled against the raging storm and the roaring seas.

Those, who were not washed overboard tried in vain to save their badly leaking boat and rapidly sinking vessel.

In describing the chaos and the confusion, the frenzy and the fear on the waterlogged and weakened 'Greyhound', John wrote:

> "..the day before our catastrophe ……I went to bed that night in my usual security and indifference but was awakened from a sound sleep by the force of a violent sea, which broke on us. Much of it came down below and filled the cabin where I lay with water. This alarm was followed by a cry from the deck that the ship was going down or sinking … while I returned for the knife, another person went up in my place, who was instantly washed overboard. We had no leisure to lament him, nor did we expect to survive him long, for we soon found the ship was filling very fast. The sea had torn away the upper timbers on one side, and made the ship a mere wreck in a few minutes … taken in all circumstances, it was astonishing and almost miraculous that any of us survived … almost every passing wave broke over my head, but we made ourselves fast with ropes, that we might not be washed away. Indeed I expected that every time the vessel descended into the sea, she would rise no more."
> (P.69-71)

For the young seaman, however, the day of salvation was here, the hour of decision had arrived, and the moment of truth was at hand. John wrote:

> "The straits of hunger, cold weariness, and the sinking (He couldn't swim) and starving, I shared with others. But besides these I felt a heart-bitterness which was properly my own. No one else on board was impressed with any sense of the hand of God in our danger and deliverance." (P.81)

With no help in sight and all hope gone, Mate Newton called on the Lord Jesus Christ in sincerity and truth, counting on the riches of His grace that saves from the gutter-most to the uttermost.

With darkness all around him, and death staring him in the face, he cried out in genuine repentance for the Redeemer's tender mercies. AND GOD SAVED HIM!

．．．．．．．．．．．．．．．．．．．．．．

AMAZING GRACE

"…I was greatly deficient in many respects…

*I had no Christian friend
or faithful minister to advise me….
I began to inquire for serious books,
but not having spiritual discernment,
I frequently made a wrong choice.*

*I was not brought up in the way of evangelical preaching
or conversation, except a few times
when I heard but understood not,
until six years later.
Those things the Lord was pleased
to show me gradually.
I learned them here a little and there a little,
by painful experience, apart from ordinary means,
and in the same evil company and bad example
I had known for some time."*

John Newton

(P.83-84)

5. Master of Slaves

After his dramatic conversion, John, a changed man, was understandably amazed at the newness of his life in Christ. He wrote:

> *"I stood in need of an Almighty Saviour, and such an one I found described in the New Testament. The Lord had wrought a marvellous thing: I was no longer an infidel. I heartily renounced my former profaneness; was seriously disposed, and sincerely touched with a sense of undeserved mercy in being brought safe through so many dangers; I was sorry for my past misspent life…; was freed from the habit of swearing which seemed to have been deeply rooted in me as a second nature. To all appearance, I was a new man."* (P.82-83)

However, his faith journey was not to be smooth sailing. His spiritual development was slow and gradual. He learned 'the things of the Lord here a little and there a little'. All in all, it took him six years to be grounded in truth and growing in grace.

His love life, on the other hand, was more successful. After 'his father paid visit to his friends in Kent, and gave his consent' for John to marry his childhood sweetheart, Mary (Polly), elder daughter of George and Elizabeth Catlett, he proposed to her in writing, since he 'always was exceedingly awkward in pleading his own cause in their conversation'.

Mary accepted and 'accordingly their hands were joined on February 1, 1750, at St. Margaret's Church in Rochester, Kent.'(P.86-87) (John Newton by Richard Cecil P.63)

As for employment, the newly married man, didn't have to look far. Considering he was born and raised in a sea captain's home, and given his extensive experience on the open sea from an early age, John naturally chose a seafaring career.

From sea-farer to slave trader

The slave trade industry, in those days, was a thriving business. John, now a sea captain in his own right, got entangled in it. Over the next four years, he commanded the following 'slave trade' trips:

From August 1750 to October 1751 - Master of the duke of Argyle Slave trader.

From June 1752 to August 1753 - Master of the African Slave trader 1st Voyage.

From October 1753 to August 1754 - Master of the African Slave trader 2nd Voyage.

In regard to slave trading, a subject that became a hot issue later on in his life, John, with his mixed up views, was confused to say the least:

On the one hand, he 'never had the least scruple as to its lawfulness'. (P.115)

On the other hand, he was 'shocked with an employment that was perpetually connected with chains, bolts and shackles'. (P.115)

In any case, he 'endeavoured to treat them with humanity, and set a good example.' He also 'established public worship, according to the liturgy twice every Lord's day'. (P.100-101)

Given his weak spiritual diet and therefore weak spiritual discernment, it's no wonder! His spiritual 'turning point' came in 1754 with the following two major events:

1. Meeting and learning from Alexander Clunie, a captain from a London ship, at St Kitts (also known as St. Christopher), West Indies. This 'instrument of good' who 'taught him from the Bible and encouraged him to pray extempore' was 'a neighbour and friend of his mother's pastor'. John wrote:

> *"...For nearly a month we spent every evening together on board each other's ship alternately and often prolonged our visits till towards daybreak. I was all ear; He not only increased my understanding, but his teaching warmed my heart. He encouraged me to open my*

mouth in social prayer; He taught me the advantage of Christian conversation; he put me upon an attempt to make my profession more public, and to venture to speak for God… and finally directed me where to apply in London for further instruction." (P.114-115)

2. Making a decision to leave the slave trade, just one day before going on a new voyage. John wrote:

"…In the afternoon as I was sitting with Mrs Newton, drinking tea, and talking over past events, I was taken by a seizure which deprived me of sense and motion, and left me no sign of life but that of breathing. It lasted about an hour. When I recovered, a pain and dizziness in my head induced the physicians to judge it would not be safe or prudent for me to proceed on the voyage. By the advice of my friend to whom the ship belonged, I resigned the command the day before she sailed." (P.116)

....

AMAZING GRACE

"At present (1763),
my desire to serve the Lord is not weakened,
but I am not hasty
to push myself forward as I was formerly.

It is sufficient that He knows
how to dispose of me,
and that He both can and will do what is best.

To Him I commend myself.

I trust that His will
and my true interest are inseparable,
to His Name be glory."

John Newton

(P.124-125)

6. Major Surrender

At the age of twenty nine, John, a growing disciple, turned his back on the sea and 'the business at which his heart now shudders', and took up a position as the tide surveyor (a custom officer) in Liverpool, England.

During this period he came to admire the earnestness of John Wesley, the founder of the Methodist movement, and the eloquence of George Whitefield, the evangelistic preacher in the Church of England.

Over the next four years, he grew in grace and in the knowledge of his Lord and Saviour Jesus Christ, as he searched the Scripture daily and studied the word diligently.

Then, in the year 1758, at the age of thirty three, sensing that God had called him to serve Him here below, John Newton surrendered his life to preach the gospel of Jesus Christ and to serve the King of Kings.

This major surrender and spiritual milestone was the fruit of his mother's dedication to his learning as a child, as well as the fulfilment of her desire for his life. He wrote:

> *"...It was my dear mother's hope that I enter the ministry. Her death, and the life in which I afterward engaged, seemed to cut off the probability."* (P.124)

The budding preacher applied to the Archbishop of York for ordination. His request was denied on the grounds that he lacked university training. John wrote:

> *"My first thought was to join the Dissenters, but preferring the Established Church in some respects, I solicited ordination from the late Archbishop of York. I need not tell you I met a refusal."* (P.124)

This action, which disgusted John Wesley, resulted in Newton ministering briefly in the Congregational church in Warwick.

Being concerned about the way the Established Church had treated him and others like him, and having considered joining the Dissenters' camp, John chose to wait patiently on the Lord for six more years.

Then, in 1764, at the age of almost forty, John was first licensed as a deacon at Buckden on April 29, and then finally ordained as a priest on June 17 by Dr Green, the Bishop of Lincoln, at the recommendation of William Legge, second Earl of Dartmouth. This good man with a 'godly disposition' was an influential patron within the Church of England.

John was appointed to the parish church of Olney. This simple country town, with a small population of approximately 2,000 dear souls, sandwiched between Bedford and Northampton near Cambridge, had an interesting spiritual history. John wrote:

> *"The gospel seed was first sown in Olney by Mr Whitefield and his brethren about the year '39... Soon after a little place was built, a society formed, and Mr Whitefield's preachers came frequently. But, in the year '54, The Lord brought Mr. Moses Brown to be Vicar. By him the gospel was preached in the church; then the Methodist preachers withdrew, and went where they were more wanted."*
> (John Newton by Richard Cecil P.265)

This is what the mighty evangelist George Whitefield wrote to Newton in response to his invitation to come and preach at Olney...

> *"Rev. and dear Sir,*
> *With great pleasure I this day read your kind letter. The contents gladdened my heart. Blessed be God, not only for calling you to a saving knowledge of Himself, but sending you forth also to proclaim the Redeemer's unsearchable riches amongst poor sinners... Gladly shall I come whenever bodily strength will allow*

to join my testimony with yours in Olney pulpit, that God is love. As yet I have not recovered from the fatigues of my American expedition. My shattered bark is scarce worth docking any more. But I would fain wear, and not rust out... " (John Newton by Richard Cecil P.131)

John loved Olney so much that, a year later, when he was offered the presidency of Whitefield's orphan-house-turned-seminary, he turned it down.

....

AMAZING GRACE

*"Perhaps thy grace may have recovered some
from an equal degree of apostasy,
infidelity, and profligacy:
but few of them have been redeemed
from a such a state of misery and depression
as I was in, upon the coast of Africa,
when thy unsought mercy
wrought for my deliverance.*

*But, such a wretch
should not only be spared and pardoned,
but reserved to the honour of preaching thy gospel,
which he had blasphemed and renounced,
and at length be placed in a very public situation
and favoured with acceptance and usefulness,
both from the pulpit and the press;
so that my poor name is known
in most parts of the world,
where there are any who know thee –
This is wonderful indeed! –
The more thou hast exalted me,
the more I ought to abase myself."*

John Newton

(John Newton by Richard Cecil P.161-162)

7. 'Mazing Song

The preacher is John Newton. He is a forty-seven-year-old curate in the parish church of St Peter and St Paul for nearly eight years. The place is Olney. It is a village of a working class and farming community, known for its bobbin-lace manufacturing and Shrove Tuesday pancake race.

1. John enjoyed a harmonious life at home

It was some 22 years since John and Mary (or Polly as she was affectionately known) were married. They were deeply in love with each other. He was her first love. She was his childhood sweetheart. He wrote:

> "My first regards for her was truly a passion, strong as ever writers of romance imagined. Neither absence, nor distance, nor the unhappy scenes of profligacy in which I was too long engaged, could extinguish it; and from the moment I had a prospect of gaining her, it sprung up with renewed force. At length the Lord gave her to me: we lived together for more than forty years in harmony, and, if possible, with increased affection." (John Newton by Richard Cecil P.80)

Polly was a vibrant, fun-loving woman who enjoyed reading and gardening. In one of her earlier letters to John, she wrote:

> "My dearest dear, ten weeks, 70 nights, 3 days since I saw you and the pleasantest half hour I have had was in dreaming I was with you the other night... Your dear letter today gave me great pleasure as indeed everyone does. But my heart went pit a pat lest you should go to Yorkshire... I like to have as much of your company as I can... The Lord bless and grant you a good day tomorrow. May your own soul be abundantly watered and may you be enabled to declare the whole counsel of God." (John Newton by Richard Cecil P.315)

The Newtons lived in the vicarage, but they also had access to a large mansion known as the Great House. According to William Cowper, the noted Hymn Writer:

> *"...the Lord seems to have filled the hearts of Mr. and Mrs. Newton with Christian tenderness and affection"*, and *"...Nothing can exceed their kindness and hospitality..."* (John Newton by Richard Cecil P.307)

11. John exercised a holy leadership in the church

John believed sincerely that *"...whenever two or three meet together in the Saviour's name, to adore him, and to praise him for his great love to sinners, the spot whereon they stand is, for the time, Holy Ground."* He also *"discovered the gift and the grace of prayer and used extempore prayer before and after his sermons; as also in his own family, and in the private houses of his friends."* (John Newton by Richard Cecil P.318)

Conservative and reformed he was, but conventional and rigid he certainly was not. (He often wore his old captain's jacket when he was out of his pulpit). John was a creative thinker and an entrepreneurial leader. Whilst his thinking did not stay inside the box, his teaching did not stray outside the Book.

His daily schedule reflected his devoted service. He was not idle, nor did he waste any time at all. He wrote:

> *"...I have seldom one hour free from interruption, letters come that must be answered, visitants that must be received, business that must be attended to, I have a good many sheep and lamb to look after, sick and afflicted souls dear to the Lord and therefore, whatever stands still, these must not be neglected ...Night comes before I'm ready for noon, and the week closes when according to the state of my business, it should not be more than Tuesday..."*
> (John Newton by Richard Cecil P.139)

Newton was an innovative preacher with plenty of initiative. He possessed a spirit of enthusiasm and promoted a standard of excellence. He searched for different means to reach the lost sinners of his community and sought dynamic methods to teach the living saints in his congregation:

• Hymn-sing

On Sundays, for instance, he and Polly invited the folk at church to come after the service to the vicarage for prayer and singing. This after-church get-together was so popular and got so big that they had to move the meeting to a bigger room in the Great House.

• Kids' Club

Long before the Sunday school movement, Newton organised special meetings for the children with suitable messages for the young. According to his authorised biographer, Rev Richard Cecil, Newton held his meeting with the children at the Great House on Thursday afternoon. On his first, 17 January, there were 49 boys and 40 girls. The attendance list over the next few weeks increased to 233.   (John Newton by Richard Cecil P.139,143)

• Midweek meeting

Newton also initiated Tuesday prayer meeting and Thursday Bible study. There he introduced his evangelical 'low Anglican' parish to new hymns and spiritual songs, many of which he personally wrote and others which he co-authored with William Cowper. These hymns were later published as the Olney Hymns. In its preface, John wrote:

> *"This publication, which, with my humble prayer to the LORD for his blessing upon it, I offer to the service and acceptance of all who love the LORD JESUS CHRIST in sincerity, of every name and in every place, into whose hands it may come; I more particularly dedicate to my dear friends in the parish and neighbourhood of Olney, for whose use the hymns were originally composed; as a testimony of the sincere love I bear them, and as a token of my gratitude to the Lord, and to them, for the comfort and satisfaction with which the discharge of my ministry among them has been attended."*

Newton and Cowper *(pronounced Cooper)* were close friends as well as co-labourers. John wrote,

> *"For nearly twelve years we were seldom separated for seven hours at a time, when we were awake, and at home: The first six I passed daily admiring and aiming to imitate him: during the second six, I walked pensively with him in the valley of the shadow of death."*
>
> (John Newton by Richard Cecil P.125)

III. John expressed a hearty love for God

It was during this season of faithful ministry, in late December of 1772, that God inspired his dedicated heart and instructed his disciplined mind to write what we now know and love as 'Amazing Grace' – originally entitled 'Faith's Review and Expectation'.

Based on the text in 1 Chronicles 17:16-17, and built on the truth of being grateful to God for past mercies and future hopes, the lyrics were prayerfully chosen, and the song was carefully written to accompany his sermon for the following New Year's Day service.

John reviewed his own life in the light of David's response and reflected on how far he had come since his seafaring days of sinful lifestyle, self-indulgence and slave trading. As he continued in deep meditation, the Vicar of Olney, like the king of Israel, was overwhelmed by God's amazing goodness and awesome greatness which brought him safe thus far.

In a spirit of humble gratitude and sincere brokenness, his wooed heart moved his willing hand to record his inner deep sense of awe with the only possible explanation that he, or any other finite and mortal human being, can utter this side of eternity.

> *'Amazing grace! (how sweet the sound)*
> *that saved a wretch like me!'*

It was right at this point that John Newton, though he didn't know it at the time, penned a hymn not just for Olney to chant, but for the world to sing.

Then, on that historic Friday morning celebration of January 1, 1773, the servant of God led the people of Olney into the New Year.

First, he read the passage of 1 Chronicles 17:16,17:
> "And David the king came and sat before the LORD, and said,
> Who am I, O LORD God, and what is mine house,
> that thou hast brought me hitherto?
> And yet this was a small thing in thine eyes, O God;
> for thou hast also spoken of thy servant's house
> for a great while to come,
> and hast regarded me according to the estate of a man of high degree,
> O LORD God."

After his usual extempore prayer, the unusual expository preacher developed the following outline:

1. The frame of mind: humility and admiration
   Who Am I?
- *Miserable*
- *Rebellion*
- *Undeserving*

2. That thou hast brought me hitherto
- *Before conversion*
- *At conversion*

3. Are these small things?
- *Love, gratitude, obedience*
- *Trust and confidence*
- *Patience*

(You can read the full message in Richard Cecil's excellent book
"John Newton - Authorised Biography" P.365-368)

Newton then concluded the service with:

1 Chronicles 17:16, 17
Faith's Review and Expectation

1. Amazing grace! (how sweet the sound)
that sav'd a wretch like me!
I once was lost but now am found,
was blind but now I see.

2. 'T was grace that taught my heart to fear,
and grace my fears reliev'd;
How precious did that grace appear,
the hour I first believ'd!

3. The Lord has promis'd good to me,
His word my hope secures;
He will my shield and portion be,
as long as life endures.

4. Thru many dangers, toils, and snares,
I have already come;
'T is grace hath brought me safe thus far,
and grace will lead me home.

5. Yes, when this flesh and heart shall fail,
and mortal life shall cease;
I shall possess, within the vail,
a life of joy and peace.

6. The earth shall soon dissolve like snow,
the sun forbear to shine;
But God, who call'd me here below,
Will be forever mine.

In 1835, 'Faith's Review and Expectation' found its soul mate in 'New Britain' and was born again as 'Amazing Grace'. A seed was conceived and a song was delivered after a spiritual message of a bold poetic truth from England's central east met and married a simple melody of an old familiar tune from America's Deep South.

Heavenly-designed and tailor-made for each other, the slave scale of five black keys suited perfectly the timeless truth of six blessed verses.

In 1900, American composer and successful publisher, Edwin Othello Excell (1851-1921) added the finishing touches with his musical arrangement. Excell also removed the final verse from the original poem and replaced it with the following stanza from "Jerusalem My Happy Home":

6. When we've been there ten thousand years,
bright shining as the sun,
We've no less days to sing God's praise
than when we'd first begun.

. . . .

.

The parish Church building, Olney

Newtons' residence, Olney

AMAZING GRACE

"That one of the most ignorant,
the most miserable,
and the most abandoned of slaves
should be plucked from the forlorn state of exile
on the coast of Africa,
and at length be appointed minister of the parish
of the magistrate of the first city in the world;
that he should there not only testify of such grace,
but stand up as a singular instance
and monument of it,
that he should be enabled to record it in his history,
preaching, and writings to the world at large,
is a fact I can contemplate with admiration,
but never sufficiently estimate."

John Newton

(P.132)

8. Ministry Of Significance

The year is 1779. John is fifty-four years of age. It has been seven productive years since he wrote 'Faith's Review and Expectation', which later became 'Amazing Grace'.

The prolific writer also 'had the honorary degree of D.D. conferred upon him by the University of New Jersey, in America, and the diploma sent him'.   (John Newton by Richard Cecil P.161)

By this stage he had published the following volumes:
* 1760 - Sermons, marked, Liverpool, January 1;
* 1762 - Omicron Letters;
* 1764 - Authentic Narrative;
* 1767 - A volume of sermons preached at Olney;
* 1769 - Review of Ecclesiastical History;
* 1779 - Olney Hymns (with William Cowper)

In addition, John Newton later wrote and/or published *Apologia, Cardiphonia, Letters to a wife, Messiah, The Christian Correspondent, Memoirs of Cowper (unfinished), Memoirs of Grimshaw,* and of course the highly controversial, *Thoughts on the African Slave Trade.*

However, the accomplished author found himself standing at a ministry crossroad and staring at a major dilemma.

Faced with unexpected opposition and frustrated by unsettling disappointments, the Newtons were forced to make a heart wrenching decision to leave the Olney community they had come to love and serve for nearly sixteen years. He wrote:

> *"My race at Olney is nearly finished. I am about to form a connection for life with one Mary Woolnoth, a reputed London saint in Lombard Street."*   (Through Many Dangers by B.H.Edwards P.218)

The veteran couple, together with Betsy, Polly's niece, whom they had adopted six years earlier, moved their home from the small village of Olney to the big city of London.

There, in the heart of its banking district, John resumed his evangelical preaching and effective ministry at the St. Mary Woolnoth Church.

His first service at the new church was on December 19, 1779. His sermon text was Ephesians 4:15:

> "But speaking the truth in love, may grow up into him in all things, which is the head, even Christ..."

As the minister reached out faithfully to his people, after 'some adjustment on the part of the regulars', the people responded favourably to his ministry. The following response to his dear friend William Wilberforce's request to move the evening service forward, so that the young politicians could attend there regularly, showed just how much his ministry was well received by the people he truly loved! He wrote,

> *"...It has pleased the Lord to give to me, the most Unworthy, much acceptance with his people. Many of my evening service hearers come from far, from most of the villages round the Metropolis... My church is full before 6, that they who are not there before the clock strikes, can with difficulty obtain a seat and by a quarter after 6 is so crowded, that many cannot get within the door... If I do not dismiss them in time for the Stage Coaches at eight o'clock, they might have to walk perhaps 3 or 4 miles home... it gives me great pain, to say, I cannot do it."* (John Newton by Richard Cecil P.202-203)

Speaking of his effective ministry, here is what Rev. William Jay, Pastor of Argyle Independent Chapel, Bath, whose period tenure stretched from Wesley to Spurgeon, said about Newton:

> *"There was nothing about him dull or gloomy, or puritanical, ...*

As he had much good-nature, so he had much pleasantry, and
frequently emitted sparks of lively wit, or rather humor... when I
asked him how he slept he instantly replied, 'I'm like a beef-steak –
once turned, and I'm done'."   (John Newton by Richard Cecil P.301)

1. Richard Johnson and Australia

John continued to be very active in the service of his Master. His new
residence in Charles Square, Hoxton, London, just like in Liverpool and
Olney, was open for spiritual counsel to all people from all walks of life
and different denominations. He wrote,

> *"I am glad of such opportunities at times to discountenance bigotry*
> *and party spirit, and to set our Dissenting brethren an example,*
> *which I think ought to be our practice towards all who love the*
> *Lord Jesus Christ and preach His Gospel without respect to forms*
> *or denominations."*   (Through Many Dangers by B.H.Edwards P.202)

In 1783, John Newton, Richard Cecil, Henry Foster and Eli Bates founded
the Eclectic Society, 'a small group of evangelical clergy and laymen'
focused on and committed to 'the practical outworking of the Christian
faith' with a particular emphasis on the new birth and the preaching of
the Gospel.

As leader of this Society, John approached Rev. Richard Johnson on
September 23, 1786 with a visionary proposal to be the chaplain and
missionary on the first fleet to the land *Down Under*. Newton was crystal
clear about the cost involved to embark on such a grand journey, and the
call required to undertake such a glorious mission. He wrote:

> *"A minister who should go to Botany Bay without a call from*
> *the Lord, and without receiving from Him an apostolic spirit, the*
> *spirit of a missionary, enabling him to forsake all, to give up all,*
> *to venture all, to put himself into the Lord's hands without reserve,*
> *to sink or swim, had better run his head against a brick wall."*
> John Newton by Richard Cecil P.178)

God blessed Newton's ministry and enlarged its boundaries from England's banking district to Australia's Botany Bay. Rev. Johnson accepted Newton's proposal, and the rest is *Australian* history. The Rev. N. K. Macintosh wrote:

> *"Richard Johnson conducted the first Christian service on Australian soil at 10 a.m. on Sunday 3 February 1788."*
>
> (The Reverend Richard Johnson by N. K. Macintosh P.8)

'The good Bishop of Botany Bay, as one of his friends (in England) jokingly called him', went on to become 'the first clergyman to minister in the Parramatta district of the infant colony of New South Wales'.

> (The Reverend Richard Johnson by N. K. Macintosh P.5 & 7)

As a fitting tribute of the chaplain's fruitful ministry, The Rev. N. K. Macintosh wrote:

> *"Newton once referred to Johnson as the Patriarch of the Southern Hemisphere, and if that seems too grand a title for one so humble, it is well to remember that he it was who planted the Gospel in Australian Soil; that he did it alone for the first few years; that he did it with virtually no support from either laymen in the colony or hierarchy at home; that he did it in the face of constant and at times almost overwhelming opposition; and that he did it in the meek, unassuming but a sensitive manner that is the true hallmark of saintliness."*
>
> (The Reverend Richard Johnson by N. K. Macintosh P.24)

II. William Wilberforce and abolishing slavery

An early work of Newton, a personal testimony entitled 'Authentic Narrative', continued to challenge more hearts for God and change many lives for good. According to John Wesley, who read this book more than once, it had 'something very extraordinary therein'. John's newly published 'Cardiphonia' (1781), and the necessarily controversial 'Thoughts on the African Slave Trade', also inspired and challenged many.

The latter helped equip and highly empowered his dear friend and beloved disciple, William Wilberforce M.P., a pro-active Christian leader and a productive, concerned parliamentarian, who after 20 years of faithful campaigning to abolish slavery, finally succeeded in 1807 in passing an act of parliament in all British colonies.

The friendship between these two history-makers went back a long way. Richard Cecil wrote:

> *"His mother (Wilberforce) placed him in the care of his aunt Hannah Wilberforce in Wimbledon after his father died. As she was the (half) sister of John Thornton, young Wilberforce saw quite a bit of John Newton both in London and in Olney and came to regard him as a father figure."* (John Newton by Richard Cecil P.174)

Their sincere friendship and strong relationship, characterised by prayer, respect, affection and trust, continued to grow and flourish as their following correspondence clearly shows:

1. Newton to Wilberforce –

> *"My heart is with you... May the wisdom that influenced Joseph and Moses, and Daniel rest upon you. Not only to guide and animate you in the line of Political Duty – but especially to keep in the habit of dependence upon God, and communion with Him... I can honestly say, that were it practicable, I should not be unwilling to travel on foot, for the sake of spending two or three days with you..."*

2. Wilberforce to Newton –

> *"I believe I can truly declare, that not a single day has passed in which you have not been in my thoughts... O my dear Sir, let not your hands cease to be lifted up, lest Amalek prevail (Exodus 17:11-16) – entreat for me that I may be enabled by divine grace to resist and subdue all the numerous enemies of my salvation. My path is peculiarly steep and difficult and dangerous, but the prize is a crown of glory and 'celestial panoply' is offered me and the God of Hosts for my ally."* (John Newton by Richard Cecil P.176-177)

III. William Carey and mission to India and beyond

Carey was the third William (Cowper and Wilberforce were the first two), whose life and ministry was greatly impacted by John Newton. This former shoemaker became passionate about evangelism after reading the journals of Captain James Cook.

Famous for his immortal quote 'Expect great things from God, Attempt great things for God', with which he urged a Baptist Association meeting at Nottingham in 1792, this young Baptist cobbler went on to become the founder and father of the modern missions movement.

Carey's connection with Newton was through the ministry of Thomas Scott and a meeting with William Wilberforce, who were both influenced by Newton. In 1821 Carey quite openly acknowledged his appreciation for the ministry of Scott:

> *"If there be anything of the word of God in my soul, I owe much of it to Scott's preaching."* (Through Many Dangers by B.H. Edwards P.213)

This is the same Thomas Scott who, following his contact and correspondence with Newton 16 years earlier, had 'publicly renounced as erroneous and grievous perversion of Scripture' his liberal thinking on the Trinity and the deity of Christ, and his rejection of the literal teaching of hell and judgment.

Carey was commended to Newton, who in turn introduced him to Wilberforce who shared his vision for world mission, and sponsored his trip to India.

On a sadder note, Mary, John's dear wife, died after a two-year battle with breast cancer on December 15, 1790. He wrote:

> *"...Wednesday evening toward seven o'clock... She began to breathe very hard... There was no start or struggle, nor a feature ruffled... I took my post by her bedside, and watched her nearly three hours,*

with a candle in my hand, till I saw her breathe her last breath, on December 15, 1790, a little before ten in the evening...When I was sure she was gone, I took off her ring, according to her repeated injunction, and put it upon my own finger. I then kneeled down with the servants who were in the room, and returned the Lord my unfeigned thanks for her deliverance, and her peaceful dismission."
(P.141-142)

John and Mary Newton's tomb

AMAZING GRACE

"JOHN NEWTON, Clerk
Once an infidel and libertine
A servant of slaves in Africa,
Was, by the rich mercy of our Lord and Saviour
JESUS CHRIST,
restored, pardoned, and appointed to preach
the Gospel he had long laboured to destroy.
He ministered,
Near sixteen years at Olney, in Bucks,
And twenty-eight years in this Church.

On February 1, 1750 he married
MARY
Daughter of the late George Catlett,
Of Chatham, Kent,
Whom he resigned to the Lord,
who gave her,
On December 15, 1790"

(The above epitaph, prepared by Newton, was placed on a plain marble tablet near the vestry door of his church. P.10)

9. Meeting the Saviour

On December 21, 1807, about 8.15 pm, at the 'right' age of eighty-two, John, a faithful servant, exited earth and entered eternity.

Newton, who used to say: 'I am packed and sealed and ready for the post', was carried by the angels, all the way beyond the blue sky, past the firmament and the beautiful stars, and right into the blessed seat of God. There, before his Chief Shepherd and the Captain of his Salvation, he was presented faultless before the presence of His glory with overwhelming joy.

Ever since Newton repented of his sin and received the Saviour, he had experienced hope on earth and was expecting heaven in eternity, The Bible says:

> "Verily, verily, I say unto you, He that heareth my word, and believeth on him that sent me, hath everlasting life, and shall not come into condemnation; but is passed from death unto life." (John 5:24)
> "We are confident, I say, and willing rather to be absent from the body, and to be present with the Lord." (2 Corinthians 5:8)

He had no doubt whatsoever about that, he wrote,

> *"Whatever I may doubt on other points, I cannot doubt whether there has been a certain gracious transaction between God and my soul. I cannot doubt whenever I look at my former and present object, whether I ought not to cry, What God has wrought!"*
> (John Newton by Richard Cecil P.380)

Newton, once having entrusted the keeping of his soul to Jesus Christ, was instantly granted hope beyond the grave and guaranteed heaven beyond the blue, just like everyone that comes to Jesus Christ by faith and calls on His precious name to be saved!

The Bible says:

> "For whosoever shall call upon the name of the Lord shall be saved."
> (Romans 10:13)
>
> "For I am in a strait betwixt two, having a desire to depart, and to be with Christ; which is far better:" (Philippians 1:23)

Hope- Beyond The Grave

As his body and heart failed and his mortal life ceased, John's soul and spirit found everlasting rest and eternal rewards inside the celestial gates of heaven. The Bible says:

> "Yea, saith the Spirit that they may rest from their labours; and their works do follow them." (Revelation 14:13)
>
> "... as it is written, eye hath not seen, nor ear heard, neither have entered into the heart of man, the things which God hath prepared for them that love him." (1 Corinthians 2:9)

Heaven - Beyond The Blue

Therefore, death for Newton was not a puzzle but a passage; not a termination but a transition. It was a means to an end, not a meaningless end. The Bible says:

> "Precious in the sight of the LORD is the death of his saints."
> (Psalm 116:15)
>
> "...Blessed are the dead which die in the Lord." (Revelation 14:13)

And God, who called him here below, is forever his!

His obituary in The Times stated, *"...his unblemished life, his amiable character, both as a man and as a minister, and his able writing, are too well known to need any comment."* (John Newton by Richard Cecil P.314)

His funeral was held on January 8, 1808, at the church of the united parishes of St Mary Woolnoth and St Mary Woolchurch Haw, Lombart Street. Rev. Richard Cecil, one of the founding members of both the Eclectic Society and the Church Missionary Society (CMS), and a very close friend of Newton, preached at the memorable service. His text was Luke 12:42-43…

> "And the Lord said, Who then is that faithful and wise steward, whom his lord shall make ruler over his household, to give them their portion of meat in due season? Blessed is that servant, whom his lord when he cometh shall find so doing."

In his message Rev. Cecil used the life of the late John Newton to illustrate *"the character and commendation of a faithful minister"*. He pointed out how Newton:

I.   As a SERVANT, was vigilant and prepared; and
II. As a STEWARD, was faithful and wise.

(You can read the full message in
Richard Cecil's excellent book "John Newton – Authorised Biography" P.376-385)

....

AMAZING GRACE

"Death, Judgement, Heaven, and Hell
are words of most importance.
But the Son of God veiled his glory ,
united the human nature to himself,
that he might redeem us to God by his blood;
and now Pardon, Peace, and eternal Life
are truly promised without money or price,
to all who put their trust in him."

John Newton

(John Newton by Richard Cecil P.348)

10. Make Sure

On his death bed, John Newton farewelled earth with this final exhortation:

"My memory is nearly gone, but I remember two things, I am a great sinner... and that Christ is a great Saviour."
(How Sweet the Sound by Noel Davidson P.265)

In these departing words, the dying preacher spontaneously but succinctly expressed what every living person must spiritually and sincerely experience, if he or she ever hopes to see and enter the throne of God's Amazing Grace in heaven.

"I am a great sinner... Christ is a great Saviour."

As we conclude this fabulous story of hope and healing, let's consider his final statement and faithful summary, which holds the key that opens the door to eternal life.

1. "I AM A GREAT SINNER"

In order to fully understand the intended meaning of the above statement, it is essential that we go back all the way to the very beginning.

When the LORD God formed man and woman from the dust of the ground, and breathed into their nostrils the breath of life, they became living souls with an outer shell (the body) and an inner spirit. (See Genesis 2:7) Created in God's likeness, the HUMAN race, the pivot of God's handiwork, was created with power and wisdom, not a 'product' that has evolved over time by chance. The Bible says:

> "And God said; Let us make man in our image, after our likeness: and let them have dominion over the fish of the sea, and over the fowl of the air, and over the cattle, and over all the earth, and over every creeping thing that creepeth upon the earth." (Genesis 1:26)

The triune God made Adam and Eve, the first male and female couple to walk on this young earth of ours, as fully-grown adults with a mature appearance.

From their state of origin in the Garden of Eden, Adam and Eve were put in charge of our one and only human race.

With the Intelligent Designer of the universe behind their name, and the innate desire for relational intimacy in their nature, Adam and Eve were built to function as social beings and were blessed to go forth and multiply.

A. The Sin of Adam
However, the life of history's first married couple whose union was made by God was eventually marred by sin.

The opening scene to their drama of dramas of the days of their lives began with the deception of Eve, followed by the disobedience of Adam. The Bible says:

> "And the LORD God commanded the man, saying, Of every tree of the garden thou mayest freely eat: But of the tree of the knowledge of good and evil, thou shalt not eat of it: for in the day that thou eatest thereof thou shalt surely die." (Genesis 2:16-17)

> "And when the woman saw that the tree was good for food, and that it was pleasant to the eyes, and a tree to be desired to make one wise, she took of the fruit thereof, and did eat, and gave also unto her husband with her; and he did eat." (Genesis 3:6)

> "And unto Adam he said, Because thou hast hearkened unto the voice of thy wife, and hast eaten of the tree, of which I commanded thee, saying, Thou shalt not eat of it: cursed is the ground for thy sake; in sorrow shalt thou eat of it all the days of thy life;" (Genesis 3:17)

This deadly choice of Adam brought with it a disastrous consequence for the whole adamic race. The natural consequence of sin was death.

Unstoppable and unbeatable, and without exemption from its consequence or escape from its condemnation, their sinful nature, their separation from God and their sentence of death automatically spread to all. The Bible says:

> "For all have sinned and come short of the glory of God. ....As it is written, There is none righteous, no, not one." (Romans 3:23; 10b)

And that's not all!
There is more bad news!

B. The Curse of the Law

The other reason why John Newton knew he was 'a great a sinner' has to do with the law, the Ten Commandments which Almighty God gave to His servant Moses:

---

1. Thou shalt have no other gods before me.
2. Thou shalt not make unto thee any graven image...
    Thou shalt not bow down thyself to them, nor serve them...
3. Thou shalt not take the name of the LORD thy God in vain...
4. Remember the Sabbath day, to keep it holy...
5. Honour thy father and thy mother...
6. Thou shalt not kill.
7. Thou shalt not commit adultery.
8. Thou shalt not steal.
9. Thou shalt not bear false witness...
10. Thou shalt not covet...

(Exodus 20:3 -17)

Divine in origin and universal in authority, the Ten Commandments:

Stand as God's good common sense and clear guideline for distinguishing right from wrong, removing the guesswork in moral behaviour;

State accurately God's basic law once and for all, and show perfectly HIS holiness and righteousness for time and eternity; and

Set out clearly God's holy standard for all humankind by which ALL of humanity – every man, woman, boy and girl in this whole wide world - will be judged on judgment day.

The Bible says:

"For whosoever shall keep the whole law, and yet offend in one point, he is guilty of all." (James 2:10)

Here is a very big problem. In the sight of God and according to His Ten Commandments, His perfect standard, you have sinned against God and broken the law – His law! We all have!!

Here is a simple test

If you have ever bowed your head or lifted your hands in prayer and worship to an idol, and/or a graven image of any size, shape, or form of anything whatsoever - then according to God's perfect standard that makes you an idolater!

If you have ever used God's name in vain and/or misused it in a frivolous, irreverent, blaspheming or a cursing manner - then according to God's perfect standard that makes you a blasphemer!

If you have ever assisted and/or committed murder of any kind including abortion - then according to God's perfect standard that makes you a murderer!

If you were ever unfaithful in your marriage and/or even looked at another woman or a man whom you're not married to and lusted after them in your heart - then according to God's perfect standard that makes you an adulterer!

If you have ever stolen anything (regardless of its value) and/or spoke

a lie to and/or about others (regardless of its colour) - then according to God's perfect standard that makes you a thief and a liar!
And so on for the rest of the laws...

This is a serious thing
The consequence of breaking God's commandments is indeed a very serious thing. The Bible says:

"And as it is appointed unto men once to die, but after this the judgment:" (Hebrews 9:27)

"...he that believeth not is condemned already..." "...the wrath of God abideth on him." (John 3: 18, 36)

"Know ye not that the unrighteous shall not inherit the kingdom of God? Be not deceived: neither fornicators, nor idolaters, nor adulterers, nor effeminate, nor abusers of themselves with mankind, nor thieves, nor covetous nor drunkards, nor revilers, nor extortioners, shall inherit the kingdom of God." (1 Corinthians 6:9-10)

"But the fearful and unbelieving, and the abominable, and murderers, and whoremongers, and sorcerers, and idolaters, and all liars, shall have their part in the lake which burneth with fire and brimstone: which is the second death." (Revelation 21:8)

So in a nutshell...
Because Adam and Eve broke
God's first commandment in the Garden of Eden,
and the entire human race broke
His Ten Commandments given on Mount Sinai,
we, the imperfect creatures and impotent sinners
that we are now,
all fail to measure up to God's standard
and therefore fall short of His glory.
Consequently there is death to face in this life
and judgement to follow in the one to come.

11. "CHRIST IS A GREAT SAVIOUR"

In the first part of his final sentence *"...I am a great sinner...",* John pointed out the consequence of the sin of Adam and the condemnation of the curse of the law. That was the bad news!

However, in the second part of his faithful statement *"... Christ is a great saviour...",* John preached the good news of Jesus Christ - His offer of forgiveness and our opportunity for repentance. The Bible says:

> "But God commendeth (demonstrates) his love towards us, in that, while we were yet sinners Christ died for us" (Romans 5:8)

A. From Heaven To Earth

With His beloved creation, i.e. you and I, separated by sin and alienated from Him, Jesus Christ, the Son of God set aside His heavenly mansion and royal throne for an earthly manger and a crown of thorns, and set out on a down-to-earth and once-for-all rescue mission to get us out of trouble with sin and the law, and to put us in touch with His grace and mercy.

With us weighing heavily on His loving heart, Jesus Christ, the Christ of God, crossed over eternity and came down to humanity, calling all to 'repent, for the kingdom of God is at hand'.

Those who call upon His name to be saved will be considered righteous and justified, having Adam's debt of sin, and its sinful deeds totally cancelled and completely taken care of.

Offering forgiveness of sin, and a home in heaven to whoever chooses to come, Jesus Christ, the Word of God, went forth with love and truth, proclaiming the best good news ever, the gospel of our salvation and of the grace and peace of God.

Having shed His blood and sacrificed His life for your sins, Jesus Christ reaches out to you, His fallen creation, to redeem (buy back) your spirit from the penalty of sin, reconcile you with the living God, restore your fellowship with the heavenly Father and reunite you with him, back into His loving arms and longing heart.

By His death and resurrection, Jesus Christ defeated the devil, destroyed his works and disarmed all of his despotic tyrannical authorities and dark spiritual forces in the universe.

B. From Law to Grace

By grace, God in Christ redeemed us all, not only from the sin of Adam, but also from the curse of the law. The Bible says:

"Christ has redeemed us from the curse of the law being made a curse for us..." (Galatians 3:13a)

The law of Moses can and will lead you to the love of Christ when you really humble yourself and repent of your sin. The Bible says:

"Wherefore the law was our schoolmaster to bring us unto Christ, that we might be justified by faith." (Galatians 3: 24)
"The Lord .... is not willing that any should perish, but that all should come to repentance." (2 Peter 3: 9)

To repent, you must acknowledge and be sorry for your sins, confess and forsake them. The Bible says;

"I acknowledge my sin unto thee, and mine iniquity have I not hid. I said, I will confess my transgressions unto the LORD; and thou forgavest the iniquity of my sin. Selah.......For I will declare mine iniquity; I will be sorry for my sin. ... Let the wicked forsake his way, and the unrighteous man his thoughts: and let him return unto the LORD, and he will have mercy upon him; and to our God, for he will abundantly pardon." (Psalm 32: 5; 38:18b; Isaiah 55:7)

May the life of John Newton, wretched sinner that he was, clearly demonstrate that no matter how deep in sin you have gone so far, God's grace is far greater still. God's Amazing Grace is all-sufficient regardless of who you are in this world and what you've done with your life.

May his inspiring story, a repentant sinner who, by God's grace, became a rejoicing winner, cause your mind to ponder over your life and legacy, and challenge your heart to prepare for your death and destiny.

May you see by faith, as Newton did, the need to appropriate, and the necessity to appreciate, the glory and riches of God's Amazing Grace. This precious gift is:

FROM GOD - "Grace be to you and peace from God the Father, and from our Lord Jesus Christ, Who gave himself for our sins, …" (Galatians 1:3-4a)

FOR ALL – "Therefore as by the offence of one judgment came upon all men to condemnation; even so by the righteousness of one the free gift came upon all men unto justification of life." (Romans 5:18)

FREE - "Being justified freely by his grace through the redemption that is in Christ Jesus:" (Romans 3:24)

FOREVER - "That as sin hath reigned unto death, even so might grace reign through righteousness unto eternal life by Jesus Christ our Lord." (Romans 5:21)

The Bible teaches that it is not in, by or through religious works, great talents, sincere feelings, natural abilities, personal strength or any self-righteous act or human effort that we are saved; it is only by the grace of God through faith in Christ alone.

This is because grace is neither from the goodness of our souls nor the greatness of ourselves. Rather, it is the gift of God. The Bible says:

"For by grace are ye saved through faith; and that not of yourselves: it is the gift of God: Not of works, lest any man should boast." (Ephesians 2:8 -9)

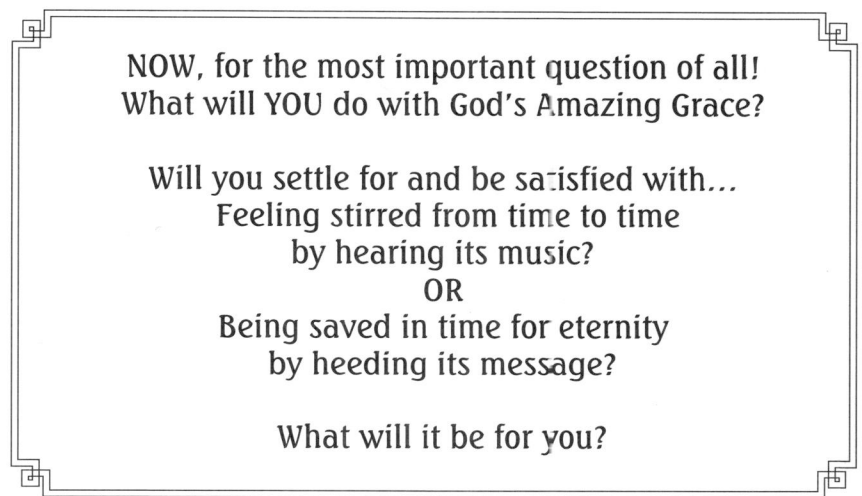

NOW, for the most important question of all!
What will YOU do with God's Amazing Grace?

Will you settle for and be satisfied with...
Feeling stirred from time to time
by hearing its music?
OR
Being saved in time for eternity
by heeding its message?

What will it be for you?

It all depends on which of the following 3 options you choose from…

1. Think about it

You've realised for the first time in your life how amazing God's grace is, and what God has done for you personally through Christ.

Something about His Amazing Grace, unconditional love, and tender mercy touched you deeply on the inside; it may even have brought sincere tears to your eyes. You found yourself nodding a few times in agreement while reading this story and you have promised yourself (and others) that you will definitely think about it.

The danger with this decision (and it is a decision) is that you will soon forget what you've read and before you know it, your soul will return to its normal position and usual setting. All that you are experiencing right now will soon wear off and simply disappear.

That's why The Bible declares with urgency:

"…To day if ye will hear his voice, harden not your hearts."

(Hebrews 3:15b)

"...Behold, now is the accepted time; behold, now is the day of salvation." (2 Corinthians 6:2b)

2. Try harder to be more religious

Perhaps you'll do more than just think about it. You commit to reviewing your life in general and renewing your religious zeal in particular. You'll do more religious things and determine to be a more religious person.

The deception with this choice is that, as nice as it may sound to you and as noble as that may seem to others, this too will fail in eternity because you are actually trusting in your good works rather than in God's grace and mercy.

The Bible warns us ALL not to rely on any works of righteousness whether the rite of circumcision or the ritual of christening to set things right with God. The only means by which sin is paid for is through the shedding of blood and the sacrificial death of Jesus Christ. The Bible says:

> "...by the works of the law there shall no flesh be justified."
> (Galatians 2:16b).

> "Not by works of righteousness which we have done, but according to his mercy he saved us, by the washing of regeneration, and renewing of the Holy Ghost;" (Titus 3:5)

Therefore do not bribe God, bargain or barter with Him, nor try to buy His salvation, for if you do, you will miss out altogether on a Father in heaven, and meet up instead with a Judge in eternity!

3. Trust Jesus right now as your Saviour and Lord

This is the third and right choice to make. Here you realise that you are a sinner and that you have broken God's law; you recognise that you can only be forgiven and saved by God's grace; and you repent of your sin by turning your back on it and your heart away from it; and you receive the Saviour by taking Him at His word and into your heart as your Saviour and Lord.

In his last will and testament dated June 13th 1803, John Newton wrote:

> *"...I commit my soul to my gracious God and Saviour... I rely with humble confidence upon the atonement, and mediation of the Lord Jesus Christ, God and Man, which I have often proposed to others, as the only foundation whereupon a sinner can build his hope, trusting that He will guard and guide me through the uncertain remainder of my life, and that He will admit me into His presence in His heavenly kingdom..."* (P.149-150)

Like John Newton, you too can commit your precious soul to Jesus Christ and confidently trust your eternal life to Him today.

Doomed without HIS grace and damned without HIS mercy, Jesus Christ is the only hope you have and the one help you need for your eternal security. The Bible says:

> "Neither is there salvation in any other: for there is none other name under heaven given among men, whereby we must be saved."
> (Acts 4:12)

> "Jesus saith unto him, I am the way, the truth and the life: no man cometh unto the Father, but by me." (John 14:6)

Jesus Christ paid for your sins in full, provided your salvation for free and promised your security forever. He now personally invites you to be saved in time for eternity.

The Bible says:

> "Come now, and let us reason together, saith the LORD: though your sins be as scarlet, they shall be as white as snow; though they be red like crimson, they shall be as wool." (Isaiah 1:18)

This lifetime offer is open to everyone who chooses to accept it. The Bible says:

"For God so loved the world that he gave his only begotten Son, that whosoever believeth in him should not perish, but have everlasting life." (John 3:16)

Like millions before you, the moment you respond to His great invitation and receive His gift of salvation you enter into a dynamic relationship with the Living God and enjoy a deep fellowship with the Loving Father.

Once received and believed, sinners are transformed into saints. Taken seriously and trusted sincerely, ordinary lay people are turned into extraordinary leaders.

The Lord of glory and the creator of humankind brought with Him His kingdom, which knows no end from heaven above to hearts within.

He is the ultimate reality in whom we find true meaning and from whom we draw full comfort. He will replace your meaningless existence with His meaningful living if you would only let Him in your heart and life.

Just as Newton sought God's mercy and was saved by God's grace, you too can call upon the Lord Jesus Christ, this very moment, and be saved in time for eternity.

To do that, the Bible makes it as simple as ABC:

Acknowledge that you are a sinner; (Psalm 32:5)
Believe that Jesus Christ died for your sins and rose again from the grave; (1 Thessalonians 4:14)
Call on His name to save you in time for eternity (Romans 10:13)

Your decision here and now on earth
will determine
your destiny there and then in Eternity!

Have you ever made this kind of decision before?

**If you cannot with all sincerity say YES,
then you must with all seriousness consider it NO!**

If you refuse and reject Jesus Christ,
You are in fact choosing to spend Eternity in hell,
But...
if you receive HIM
you will spend Eternity in heaven and rejoice evermore.

*The following simple prayer is the most important request
you'll ever ask God for in your lifetime!*

*Dear Lord God,
I am sorry that I have sinned against You
and broken Your Commandments.
I turn away from my sins.
Please forgive me, and be merciful to me a sinner.
I believe Jesus Christ died for my sins
and rose from the dead.
I now receive You, Lord Jesus,
into my heart as my Saviour and Lord.
Thank You dear Lord for giving me
a new and eternal life.
I invite You to live Your life through me
and to make me the person that You want me to be.
In Jesus Name, I pray,
Amen*

GO IN PEACE, GROW IN GRACE

Come now today, from near and far,
Come to the Saviour, just as you are.
He died for you, on Calvary.
His precious blood will set you free,
And saves you for eternity.
Receive freely,
His grace, love and mercy

Then go in peace, grow in grace,
Your new master, give him first place,
Love him so, with all your might.
Walk by faith and not by sight,
Trust him in your darkest night,
And be true
In what you think, say or do.

Keep looking up, the Lord of Lords
Is coming back with His rewards.
Serve patiently, He won't be long,
But until then, in Him be strong,
When you're feeling down,
Sing a new song,
Give thanks and pray,
And rejoice every day.

(Words & Music – Peter Rahme)

Staying in Touch

If you found this book helpful in any way and you want to find out how to:
(Please tick the appropriate box/es)

☐   Grow in Grace
☐   Order more copies for family or friends
☐   Order the Gospel tract version
☐   Order the Audio version
☐   Order the story on an A3 poster
☐   Order the companion note book
☐   Donate to 'the Libraries of the World Outreach Fund'

☐   Other: _____

Feel free to jot down your name and address on this form or email us on the address below. We would enjoy hearing from you.
(Please print your details)

Name: _____

Address: _____

City: _____ State /Province: _____

Zip / Postcode:_____ Country: _____

Tel: (   )_____ Fax: (   )_____

Email: _____

Website:_____

Mail to:
Amazing Grace - P.O. Box 5296 Chullora NSW 2190 AUSTRALIA
Tel (+61 2) 9742 5716; Fax (+61 2) 9742 5715
Website: www.amazinggrace.org.au
Email: info@amazinggrace.org.au

Also by Peter Rahme

Gospel Leaflets/Tracts
- The Pain & Gain of Adversity
- The Life & Legacy of Mr Eternity
- The Provision & Purpose of Grace
- The Power & The Passion of Christ
- The Glory & Grace of Jesus Christ
- The Loving & Lacking of Discipline
- The Peace & Prosperity of Jerusalem
- The Desire & Design for Reconciliation
- The Man & The Story Behind Amazing Grace
- The Errors & Inaccuracies of the Da Vinci Code

Sermon Series /Booklets
- The Grace & Peace of God
- The Cause & Cure of Death
- The Life & Legacy of Mr Eternity
- The Glory & Grace of Jesus Christ
- The Sign & Fulfilment of Isaiah 7:14
- The Service & Rewards of The King
- The Person & Power of the Holy Spirit
- The Leadership & Success of Nehemiah
- The Appointment & Appearance in Eternity

Audio Tapes /CDs
- Even So Come Lord Jesus (22 Original Songs)
- I will Greatly Rejoice in the Lord (20 Original Songs)
- The Man & The Message behind Mr. Eternity
- The Man & The Story Behind Amazing Grace
- The Life & Legacy of Mr Eternity (Original Song/Story)